TO YOU FROM ME

Folk Verse by
Melba Hughes

RAINBOW BOOKS • MOORE HAVEN, FLORIDA

TO YOU FROM ME, FOLK VERSE
BY MELBA HUGHES
Copyright 1987/All rights reserved

Produced by Ratzlaff & Associates
Cover Design by Danny Atchley

Published by Rainbow Books/Betty Wright
2299 Riverside Drive/P.O. Box 1069
Moore Haven, FL 33471

Library of Congress
Card Catalogue No.: 86-63961
ISBN: 0-935834-56-7
Retail Price: $6.95

Printed in the United States of America

CONTENTS

A Child's Anticipation Of Spring 54
A Dubious Tale 50
A Lesson In Humility 59
A Little Boy's Dream 13
A Mother's Prayer 55
Aged Gardener 53
Adversity 25
Aunt Sue 47
Christmas Night 35
Condescension 54
Ecstasy Of Love 18
Ephemeral Delight 55
Final Arrangements 32
Ghost Of Mount Vernon 14
His Voice 53
I' ll Wear A White Rose 19
In Time Of Tears 65
Letter To A Friend 36
Life's Lesson 56
Love's Gift 52
Loving Patience 25
Mom 40
My House By The Sea 20
My Human Side 39
My Quest 46
No Christmas 57
No Time To Write 67
Old Man In The Homespun Shirt 7
Old Squaw's Revenge 38
Our Child 16
Reflected Image 34

Reflection	66
Second Thoughts	60
Simple Things	61
Snow Storm In Montana	26
Spirit Of Determination	37
Sugar Lyle	41
Take Note	24
Tell Me, Mary	17
The Day My Grandpa Died	10
The Family	52
The Relic	68
The Valentine	66
To My Friend	35
To My Reader	6
Unknown Intercessor	18
What Might Have Been	62
World Traveler	58

To My Reader

This little volume is my tombstone.
I've thought about it — What care I
For a shaft of cold white marble
When I die?

Though mistakes I've made and many,
Wrong as sin I've often been,
Yet I want my life recorded
In the hearts of men.

"By their fruits ye shall know them."
Know ye me. When I depart
Much preferred to shafts of marble
Are epitaphs written on the heart.

Old Man In The Homespun Shirt

When I was twelve my dad said, "Son,
We'll go to town when week is done.
We'll take the buggy and the mare.
I have some business to do there."

And so it was that bright spring day
We passed a wagon on the way.
A grey-haired man, I well recall,
In homespun shirt and overalls,
Sat upon the driver's seat
With brogan shoes on his feet.

We trotted right on past his team,
Feeling our own self-esteem,
For our new rig and silky mare
Were far beyond his to compare,

We proudly rode on in to town;
Men looked our rig up and down.
The courthouse square was where we tied.
Next to the bank we went inside.

A big new sign above the door
Replaced the one there before.
FORD MOTOR COMPANY — (a strange new sound)
Told folks the horseless carriage had come to town.
We walked on past the showroom floor
Back to the open office door.

The dealer there in business clothes
Looked the part from head to toes.
He asked my dad, "How are you, Frank?"
And introduced a salesman, Hank.
My dad explained he came to pay
For a wagon that he bought in May.

When this was done they got some kicks
From telling jokes and politics.
About this time all eyes centered
On the front door where someone entered.
I was surprised as there in strode
The man we passed back down the road.

An old cliche, "as poor as dirt,"
Spoke loudly from his homespun shirt.
But none the less, he walked straight to
The latest model of the new.
He looked incongruous as he stood
By the automobile with the polished hood.

The dealer flicked his big cigar
And said to Hank, "Go sell that car."
So Hank, the salesman, ambled off
And condescending with a cough,
Said, "You're a farmer, so I guess?"
The old man smiled and said, "Oh, yes.
I have a farm just out of town
Where I still like to putter 'round."

Not a word of information
Or of salesman's oration
Did Hank offer to the man.
He just let the old man stand.
Soon he came back to listen in
To what my dad said to his friend.

The dealer asked, "What did he say?"
"Oh, we just passed the time of day,"
Said Hank, then added, "It's remote
If that old man could buy a goat."

I thought the dealer then would faint
He was so outraged with Hank.
"I'll have you know that's Paul Russ.
He owns the bank and the bank owns us."
With that he left Hank, Dad, and me
And went to the man and the Model-T.

They talked a bit, in a business way,
Then I heard what the old man had to say.
"My son's at Harvard; he's passed the bar;
When he gets home he'll need a car.
I thought it would be a nice surprise
To have one waiting when he arrives."

So the sale was made by the words, "I'll buy."
And I heard Hank mutter, "Next time I'll try."
I often think of that man named Paul
In the homespun shirt when I recall
The day I happened to discover
It's foolish to judge a book by its cover.

The Day My Grandpa Died

I was only ten years old
    When Grandpa died
But I recall the loss I felt
    And how I cried.
I went down to the barn
    Up in the hay
And nursed my unaccustomed grief
    Throughout the day.

Grandpa had been the one
    To whom I'd gone
With major problems that
    I couldn't solve alone
Like broken bikes;
    A tangled fishing line;
A kite tail overhead
    Caught in a pine.
He solved them all
    Like grandpas do
With patience
    And a loving word or two.

He sat me on a horse
>	When I was four,
As Grandma watched us
>	From the kitchen door,
And led the horse slowly
>	Down the lane
While I sat bareback
>	Holding to the rein.

And later on
>	He took me to a creek
And taught me how to swim.
>	It took a week.
He said, "With perseverance
>	I'm sure that you
Will swim the stream
>	Before the week is through."
When I dog-paddled
>	To the other side
We both laughed
>	And shared our mutual pride.

As I lay there
    Upon the hay that day
My young life seemed
    In dismal disarray.
Cicero found me when he came
    To feed the stock.
He said, "Boy, you got to eat;
    You can't lay here in shock.
We have to learn to carry on.
    Now understand
You ain't a child no more . . .
    You got to be a man.
I lost my ma and pa
    Two days apart,"
He said, "They died of influenza;
    It broke my heart."

And I could tell,
    Though he did not cry,
And he was big and black,
    He felt the same as I.
But since that day
    I have never cried.
I guess that I grew up
    The day my grandpa died.

A Little Boy's Dream

I have one wish before I die
To fly a jet up in the sky.
I'd turn and roll and break the sound
And awe spectators on the ground.
I'd go to right and then to left
They'd yell, "He's going to kill himself."
And while they watched I wouldn't stop
I'd spin that plane just like a top.
I'd zoom straight down but 'fore I hit
I'd pull that plane right out of it.
Then up into the clouds I'd soar
And come back faster than before.
I'd write my name across the sky
In smoking letters ten feet high.
They'd read and say, "He's quite an ace."
(There'd be a smile across my face.)
I'd whiz by so low they'd duck;
Some might think that lightening struck.
I'd scare 'em but I wouldn't care.
I'd just buzz and burn the air.
I'd make 'em gasp with disbelief
As they watched my expertise.
They'd have a firetruck standing by
In case my plane dropped from the sky.
But I'd land safely back on earth
And really show'em what I'm worth.

Why do I rave with all this talk?
Perhaps because I cannot walk.

Ghosts of Mount Vernon

I was walking past Mount Vernon
After midnight; all was quiet
When I heard the sound of voices
Coming to me through the night.

So I stopped and quietly listened
Feeling much more guilt than fear
For I knew the conversation
Wasn't meant for me to hear.

"George," the sweet voice of a woman
Came from not too far away,
"Did you see all those people
Who came to our house today?"

Then I glimpsed a female figure
In the shadows by the gate
But her costume, although lovely,
Was uniquely out of date.

"Yes, dear Martha," came distinctly,
Like three words upon the breeze.
Then a tall and ghostly figure
Moved behind a clump of trees.

Gee, I thought, can I be dreaming
Am I not awake and sane?
I was more confused than ever
When I heard the voice again.

"Yes, the crowd was quite unusual
And all along throughout the day
It was interesting to listen
To what the people had to say.

There was one, a British colonel
And he spoke right well of us.
That seemed odd when I remembered
All that revolution fuss.

And some silly thing was mentioned
About my father's cherry tree;
It seemed that incident reflected
On my own veracity.

There was one man by the river
Who was somewhat of a bore.
In attempts to be facetious
He called me a discus thrower.

It seems a bit ironic
That the stores I like best
Are a few things I remember
That somehow never got to press.

Like one thing no one mentioned,
An incident of note,
The night we crossed the Delaware
We all but sank the boat."

About this time a pebble
Made a sound beneath my shoe.
For a second all was silent
And I wondered if they knew.

Sure enough Martha heard it
For she made one last remark,
"George, I have this eerie feeling
There's someone out there in the dark."

Our Child

He has your eyes and gentle smile
Yet there are times I see
A lot about this child
That looks like me.

His profile; the nose, the chin,
In fact most every line
If traced, would prove to be
A miniature of mine.

But these things are genetic —
The miracle is that he
Is God's own special gift
To you and me.

Tell Me, Mary

Mary, did you know
>the night your Son was born
That He would someday wear
>a crown of thorns?

When you, His mother, kissed His cheek
>and held His tiny hand
Did God reveal
>the secret of His plan?

When wise men came
>and called your baby King
And shepherds heard
>the heavenly angels sing
Did your own heart
>in aching silence cry
To know that men
>would someday shout, "Crucify."

Then by His resurrection
>your Son would conquer sin.
Tell me, Mary
>did you know then?

Unknown Intercessor

A saddened heart bent low my head
My tears had fallen free
All through the day into the night
My grief had followed me.

But when I laid my head to rest
It seemed so very clear
That in a sweet and gentle way
My Lord was drawing near.

Then as I felt His healing Power
I knew it had to be
That in my dark and lonely hour
Someone had prayed for me.

Ecstasy Of Love

I never dreamed that life could be so sweet
Or that my spirit on a cloud could soar
Or that my heart with rapture e'er would beat
'Til you, my dear, came through the door.

But from the moment that my eyes met your's
Across the distance of a crowded room
I understood the pain that love endures
To reach maturity like a rose in bloom.

I'll Wear A White Rose

On Mother's Day I'll wear a white rose
From a bush my mother grew.
I'll go to church and pray with those
Dear friends my mother knew.

I'll hear a message on mother love
And it will bring to mind
The memories of a virtuous one . . .
That dear sweet mom of mine.

In memory I'll hear my mother's voice
And see her gentle smile.
I'll feel the touch of her loving hand
When I was a little child.

I'll recall that she spoke of another Home
Where angel's robes are shining bright;
On Mother's Day, for the very first time,
I'll wear a rose of white.

My House By The Sea

Castles and palaces are not for me
I want a cottage beside the sea
Built of timbers, mortar, and stone
As strong as the rock that it's built on.
I'd like a fireplace in the den
To burn driftwood that the tide brings in.
My house would be a comfortable place
With its unique style of charm and grace.
An overstuffed chair beside the hearth
In tones of green, or maybe earth,
Would beckon me when day was through
To sit and read, as bookworms do.
I'd have good books to fill one wall
And a set of Shakespeare in the hall.
For it's said of men you can tell their breed
Unquestionably, by the books they read.
I'd make a concession to luxury
With my silver service for coffee and tea.
It would grace a low fireside table.
It's an old heirloom from my grandmother Gable.
If it could speak it could tell me tales
Of hospitality to the Prince of Wales,
For it once belonged to a British peer.
His daughter, Anne, brought it here.
Across the room would be my desk
And over it would hang a crest
That represents my family line.
It's a gift from an artist friend of mine.

I have a quaint old German clock
That measures time tick tock, tick tock.
Balanced by a Bombay candle
It would rest on the left end of the mantle.

I think it relevant to mention here
I have a dog I hold quite dear.
He's a big German Shepherd that I call Tramp.
I found him one night cold and damp.
He was shivering and hungry; a little lost pup.
He seemed quite grateful when I picked him up.
He needed care, so I took him in.
He's been my companion ever since then.
So in this house, there he, too, would be
In front of the hearth or close by my knee.
Though he might not know it, he'd be co-owner
Of every room, closet, and corner.
I can see this house, with its weathered look
Like a haven of rest in a story book,
With a picture window facing south
And a view of the beach and an old lighthouse.

The keeper there would be my friend.
We'd share a lot and feel a-kin.
Sometimes in the early light of day
I'd go for a walk and look his way.
I'd see him there moving about;
A lonely figure, going in or out.
There'd be times when he'd see me, too.
He'd wave and call, "How are you?
Come up for coffee, it's fresh brewed."
So I would go, being in the mood.

We'd sit and chat about the weather
Or speculate if, or whether,
The fishermen would get their haul
Or be forced in by a sudden squall.
But I'd go back to my own place
And leave him his day and work to face.
But having talked, we'd both feel good
In that special way real neighbors would.

There'd be bright days with clear blue skies
When ships were visable several miles,
When gentle waves caressed the shore
Beneath the sky where seagulls soar.
These days I'd walk along the beach
And study lessons tides can teach.
Perhaps I'd pitch a stick to sea
And Tramp would bring it back to me.

I'm sure I'd like this placid life
Away from city noise and strife.
But I don't underestimate
The hardships I would not escape.
For there would be northeastern gales
That lash the seas and seldom fails
To come ashore along the coast
And with its fury cast its most
Ferocious storms upon the land
Trying the very heart of man.
In times like these I'd settle down
To Dickens' tales of Londontown.

And as the storm spent its wrath
Along its vicious inland path
I'd sample Puerto Rican rum
And toast the friend that it came from.

As foghorns droned through wind and rain
And thunder clashed near our domain
I'd notice Tramp perk up his ears
And sensing his disquieting fears
I'd stroke his head and gently say,
"Don't worry, boy. Everything's OK."
Then he'd edge closer to my knee
To tell me that he trusted me.

Throughout the storm, each hour or so,
I'd use a two-way radio
And ask my friend, "Are you OK?"
He'd answer, "Yes," and then he'd say,
"I've been in touch with Boston's tower.
They said perhaps within the hour
The worst would pass: it's calming there
But we have yet the worst to bear.
By morning we can just expect
This area here to be a wreck."
With that he'd turn it back to me.
I'd say, "We'll have to wait and see."
But I would know, by driving rain
Against my seaward window pane,
That he was right — we'd have a mess.
His wasn't just a hazard guess.

The storm would pass, they always do,
But we would know, between us two,
By having shared the season's weather
We'd grown a closer bond together.

So in this way my life would pass
For nothing in this world will last,
But even then I'd like to be
Near my house beside the sea.

Take Note

All of us are ignorant
Only in different ways . . .
A city-bred New Yorker
Wouldn't know a jack-ass brays.

Conversely, a common cowpoke
Whose wisdom serves him well
Wouldn't understand the language
Of a Wall Street cartel.

So when your ego rises
Because of what you know
Be careful of your subject . . .
Your ignorance might show.

Adversity

Adversity is the mountain
That I must climb to reach
The height of understanding
That only it can teach.

Smooth sailing on the water
Near islands fair and warm
Does not teach the sailor
To cope with raging storm.

May I not shrink the trials
That tend my soul to tire
For clay is easily shattered
That has not felt the fire.

Loving Patience

A blighted soul once came my way
And God admonished me,
"You are your brother's keeper.
Show him eternity."

It took five years to make a dent
But when his eyes were wide
He opened up his heart to God;
Today, a saint, he died.

Snow Storm In Montana

We went to bed about half past ten
It must have started snowing then;
I think it snowed throughout the night;
By morning our whole world was white.
When we awoke at early dawn
Our stallion and two mares were gone.
I guess I failed to latch the gate
The night before for it was late
When I finished with my chores,
Left the barn and went indoors.

At any rate the stock was out
And after looking all about
I thought I'd better track them down
Across the hills of frozen ground.

I bundled up in heavy clothes
From top of head down to my toes,
Strapped my rifle on my back
And started looking for a track.

I left the house at eight o'clock
Thinking that my precious stock
Could not have strayed so far away;
I'd be back without delay.

I followed tracks for quite a while;
The distance, roughly, about a mile,
Then it began to snow again
Fouling up my rescue plan.
As horses tracks began to fade
Snow also filled the tracks I made.

At this time it began to drift
And it became quite hard to lift
Each weary foot from deep in snow
As farther on I tried to go.

Since I could see no further tracks
I wondered if I should turn back
But thinking surely pretty soon
I'd find the stock, at least by noon,
I ventured on another hour
Toward where I thought was the tower.

When I arrived about the place
I thought it was, there was no trace
Of anything I recognized.
At this time, humbly, I surmised
That I was lost; I didn't know
The faintest way in which to go.

I looked around from left to right;
Everything I saw was white.
The snow was falling in big flakes
Blotting out the whole landscape.
I could barely tell east from west
So I walked up to the crest
Of a hill and tried to see
Some familiar bush or tree.

But the snow was like a curtain
And I knew, now for certain,
That my life was in some danger;
Somewhat odd for me, a rancher.
By now I was getting tired,
Feeling hungry, and desired
Something to restore my strength
If this was going on at length.

I thought perhaps I'd shoot a hare
(It wouldn't be my usual fare)
But I hadn't seen a one
Since the day had first begun.
But I took my trusty rifle
From my back and tried to stifle
Any thought of grave disaster
In this vast expanse of pasture.

I began an earnest search
For a bird upon a perch
Or a rabbit unaware
Of my intruding presence there.
I wandered 'round all afternoon;
I knew that now, pretty soon,
Night would fall; my fate it seal.
I really had to have a meal.

By four o'clock I felt quite beaten;
It had been hours since I had eaten.
I had covered much terrain
Yet it all had been in vain.

I sat down upon my rump
By a weatherbeaten stump;
Laid my gun down by my side,
While a bootlace I re-tied.
While I sat there on the ground
There came a distant barking sound.
As I listened to what I heard
Something very strange occurred.

Like a picture clearly drawn
There appeared a little fawn,
Looking at me in surprise
Out of innocent big brown eyes.
He just looked at me in wonder
And I thought, "How did you blunder
Into such a situation?
You're such a lovely creation."

With the faith of a beseecher
I just knew God sent this creature
To prolong and save my life
So I could get home to my wife.

I raised my gun with marksman's skill
With an aim I knew would kill
But I couldn't pull the trigger
At the innocent little figure.

He stood quite still; no sign of fear
As though he knew his mission here.
He looked demure, one front foot lifted;
I thought, "My dear, how gracefully gifted."
For just a bit he waited there
With one last, long wide-eyed stare.
Then he turned and walked away
Through the snow that fell that day.

When the deer was out of sight
I again thought of my plight.
I cursed myself, (that's not my rule)
For having been such a fool.
How was God going to save me
If I refused what He gave me?
With a sudden change of mind
The deer, I knew, I had to find.

He had gone off down the hill
And I thought he'd be there still.
So I followed in his track
Thinking I would get him back.

It was twilight, soon to be
Much too dark for me to see.
I hurried on along the trail
Where last I saw his white-tipped tail.

But he was gone — clear out of sight
And it seemed I'd spend the night
There alone — I felt dispair.
I even said a little prayer.
But something told me to go on,
Even though the deer was gone.
It was like an inner voice
Urging me to make that choice.

I stumbled on, a yard or two,
Not really knowing what to do.
I passed some firs, thick and dense,
And then, BEHOLD! I saw a fence!
The very fence I built last May.
I knew the fence. I KNEW THE WAY!

I was home by six o'clock
And, of course, there was my stock.
My horses used horse's sense;
I had to use the fence.

There's a moral to this story
Of this northwest territory.
Sometimes we misunderstand
The meaning of God's guiding hand.
He only sent the fawn to LEAD me
When I thought He meant to feed me.

Final Arrangements

Three hobo tramps sat late one night
In shadows of a campfire light.
They shared their beans, their bread, and bacon
And talked of things like alms they'd taken.

But with the mood that midnight brings
Their talk turned to graver things.
Joe said, "Sometimes I think of when
This worldly life of mine will end.

"I'd like to know the undertaker
Will dress me up to meet my Maker.
I want someone to shave this beard
For I don't want to look so weird;
I've always wanted to look neat
In the presence of St. Pete.

"I'd be happy if I knew
They'd lay me out in navy blue,
A red rosebud in my lapel —
The kind the better florists sell.

"I want my casket lined with silk —
Kind o' creamy; about like milk.
I'd like handles made of gold —
The finest thing the company sold.

"I vision flowers all about
My casket and the church throughout;
At least a hundred wreathes or more
And ushers standing at the door."

Mike interrupted, "Tell us, Joe,
Where you gonna get that dough?"
"I guess," he said, "When all is done
They'll pay it from the county fund."

But Pat had a different view,
"Well, that's alright for you,
But I won't consider it unkind,
In fact, with me, it will be fine,
If two good ole boys about half drunk
Stuff me in a rusty trunk
And cart me off out of town
And put my carcass in the ground.
The trunk, they'd probably have to steal,
But I'd rest fine in potter's field
For I won't know a thing the day
That I am dead and put away."

Then Mike spoke up, "I'm on my way
Back to a place near Santa Fe
Where I'll finish up my life
Whittling trinkets with my knife.

"But I have no kith or kin —
Nobody like a lifelong friend,
But I have a bit of land
And I've devised myself a plan.
I'll dig a grave long and deep
And when I'm ready for that sleep
I'll go out and lay me down
By the opening in the ground.
When I know that I'm near death
I'll turn and roll with my last breath
Into the hole, then perchance,
I'm covered with an avalanche
Of dirt and sod. The job complete;
O'er my grave the grass can creep.

    Folks might laugh
When they read my epitaph;

'Here lies Mike; no kin he left;
When he died he buried himself.'"

Reflected Image

Like silver refined to its brightest gleam
Mirrors an image true and perfectly,
So cleanse my heart, Oh, God, that others see
Christ's sweet love reflected in me.

                      Ref. Malachi 3:3

Christmas Night

A million stars shine down on the snow;
In all the windows candles glow.
I stand alone by a tall streetlight
Enjoying the beauty of Christmas Night.

The hustle and bustle has come and gone;
Gifts were opened at early dawn.
The rush is over; all is quiet;
How sweet is the world on Christmas Night!

I vision shepherds awake in a field;
I see Joseph and Mary to a manger steal.
The shepherds I witness follow a light
To find the Glory of Christmas Night.

To My Friend

You've been a special blessing
How good of God to send
A loving, caring person
Like you to be my friend!

When life ebbs low with sorrow
When dark clouds hide the sun
And you're in need of someone near
Please let me be the one.

Letter To A Friend
Dedicated to Dottie Hammett
Alexandria, VA

It's been a while since I have heard
Just how you are. I'd like a word
Telling me that you're OK.
I wish that word would come today.

Or better still pick up the 'phone
And call one day when you're alone
Tell me how the children are
And if you've had to trade your car.

I think of you so often now
Since you have moved and wonder how
I would have managed in past years
Without your help in time of tears.

Remember when the kids were small
The circus came; we took them all
And one got lost? I thought I'd die.
You were calm; I had to cry.

And when my Henry lost his job
I can't forget how you and Bob
Went overboard to help us out —
Said that's what friendship's all about.

The neighbors here are nice, and yet —
There's just no way I can forget
The things you did — the way you cared
And all the good and bad we shared.

There'll never be a neighbor who
Can be a better friend than you.
I send my love and wait to hear
Just how you are. Please write, my dear.

Spirit of Determination

A rocking chair waits over there
I do not need it, I declare.
Although I'm eighty I shall wait
Until a future fateful date.

A walking cane hangs on the wall
To help me if I tend to fall,
But I pass it with disdain;
I do not want a walking cane.

When I no longer get about
To do my duties in and out,
Reluctantly, I may give in
But it shall be with much chagrin.

Old Squaw's Revenge

I once heard a story
That I wondered could be true
It's what American Indians
To their old squaws used to do.
When they were aged and duties
They no longer could assume
They sent them in a dugout
Down the river to their doom.

I asked an Indian friend
If he really knew the facts.
He said he heard a story
But confirmation lacks.
"The legend goes a tribe
Sent a grandma to her fate
Down a white-water river
Back in Seventeen-Sixty-Eight.

But the next night a fire came
As midnight rolled around,
Swept through the camp suspiciously
And burned the teepees down.
They all said, 'Grandma's spirit
To our village has returned.'
But I believe, if truth were known,
It was she their teepees burned.

For I had an old ancestor
Who lived where the river bent.
He found a dugout on a white sandbar
And the tracks of a squaw's footprint."

My Human Side

I have a side that's human;
It points to each mistake,
However unimportant,
That friends and neighbors make.

It sometimes reacts badly
To petty little things,
Standing in the way
Of joy that friendship brings.

But there's another side
That God has given me
That He wants me to show
To all humanity.

It's selflessness and laughter;
A heart that's good and true.
Lord, help me project
The side that speaks of You.

Mom
(In memory of Helen Hughes)

Mom, dear Mom, if you but knew
How much your family misses you!
We've always known God blessed the day
He sent you here to pave our way.

He must have told the angels there,
"This one is special; I took the care
To cast her in a unique mold
And put in her a heart of gold.
I've taken stardust from the skies
And sprinkled in her loving eyes.
A sunbeam caught from heaven's air
Was touched lightly to her hair.
Another thing I thought worthwhile —
I gave to her an angel's smile.
And from a rose I took the dew
To make her tears; I'm sure that you
Will understand this special one
Must be returned when life is done.
Her gentle ways will always bless
Those nearest her with happiness.

It's almost time now for her birth —
Take her gently down to earth.
And since I've finished for the day
I'll just throw this mold away."

Sugar Lyle

I asked my ma, a coal black slave,
Why my skin was so light
And why my hair was softly waved
While her's was curly tight.

She looked across plantation fields
With cotton white as snow,
Wiped her sweat-drenched brow and said,
"I guess God willed it so."

But even then, at eight years old,
Not satisfied, I said,
"Ma, I'm old enough to know;
Is my papa dead?"

Then she told me a story
Of a young man fair and tall
Who spent a week's vacation
At the manor, Moore's Hall.

She said she did his laundry
And found favor in his sight
And in the shadows of the moon
He came to her one night.

But on the morrow he was gone . . .
In time she bore his child,
Light of skin with wavy hair;
She named me Sugar Lyle.

So I grew up with visions
Of my father tall and fair.
I felt that someday we would meet
And he would surely care.

But I was born a slave child
Like my mother was before
And worked from dawn to dusk
For my owner, Master Moore.

He was a cruel and heartless man
And many a lash he gave
For nothing more than being slow
To any who was his slave.

My mother died when I was twelve
And even though I tried
To do the work and fill her shoes
He was not satisfied.

The years passed by swiftly;
The day I was sixteen
I had a fight with Master Moore
That bordered on obscene.

I'd over slept that morning
And was standing almost nude
When he came bursting through the door
In a raging mood.

He shoved me down across the bed
And lashed me with his whip;
When I fought furiously back at him
The whip stock cut my lip.

Then as he slapped my bleeding face
I screamed defiantly,
"If my pa was here
You wouldn't do this to me."

I thought the man was going to faint;
He stopped and dropped his head.
Without another word he left;
I fell across the bed.

I did not go to work that day;
Just stayed there in my shack.
I really meant to kill him
If he, that day, came back.

But Fate plays a roll in life
We seldom understand
And so it did between myself
And this tyrant of a man.

He owned a big white stallion
With spirit wild and free;
His two rebellious chattels
Were the stallion and me.

I fed the big horse apples
And sometimes sugar, too.
We understood each other
Like kindred spirits do.

No one had ever conquered
This equine's regal pride
But Master Moore determined
To saddle him and ride.

I heard a great commotion
Down by the old lot gate
And looking out I realized
The man had met his mate.

Master Moore was striving
His supremacy to declare;
The horse's nostrils flaring,
Front feet high in the air.

The man jerked on the bridle
The horse's hoofs came down
With force like crashing thunder;
The man lay on the ground.

I ran screaming to the rescue
And drove the horse away
And kneeling by my master
My heart just seemed to say,
"Oh, God, forgive this man;
Forgive his every sin,
And cleanse my heart as well
Before his life shall end."

His blue eyes opened briefly;
His words touched on remorse,
"Lyle, you're both alike;
I'm giving you the horse."

His head, I craddled in my arms
And in my arms he died.
Long will I remember
His face so satisfied.

When his rites were over
His sweet wife generously
Came to my shack and said
That she was freeing me.

We talked about my mother
And all that she had said
About my handsome father
When I asked if he was dead.

She reached and took my hand in her's
And with a gentle smile
Said, "Your mother made up that story;
You are my husband's child.
And I'd like to share together
Our future good or bad
If you will be the daughter
That I never had."

My Quest

I searched for God in a troubled hour;
I found His fingerprint on a flower.

I looked for Him upon the seas;
I felt His breath in an ocean breeze.

I asked my God to speak to me;
I heard His voice in a bird's melody.

I knew my quest must never stop;
Then I felt His presence on a mountain top.

Aunt Sue

I still remember seeing her cry
But I was too young to know just why.
I can see her working about the place
With tears trickling down her face.
She never left a thing undone
From early morn till setting sun,
And even then, sometimes till late
She worked at things that couldn't wait.

She was mama's sister; my Aunt Sue.
She had two kids; three and two.
We were always in and out
Before the crisis came about.

When I was older I learned, of course,
Uncle John had asked for a divorce.
He wanted to marry the widow Gray
Who owned a farm down the way.

I remember the day he left;
She called and said, "I'm by myself
With just the kids; he won't be back."
Right then my mom began to pack
And we went out to stay with them
Till she got over losing him.

It wasn't easy for her to part
With the man she loved with all her heart,
But after weeks of grief and pain
She somehow seemed herself again.
But I believe that deep inside
She loved him till the day she died.

For there were times in later years
When I saw her close to tears.
One Sunday morning she and I
Saw his family passing by;
They looked quite happy on their way
To a local church on Mother's Day.
She turned her head; I saw the pain
In her troubled eyes again.

The years went by — ten or more,
Then Uncle John knocked on her door.
"Sue," he began, and dropped his head,
"My wife, Mary, is nearly dead.
She has the fever; I thought that you
Might come and help me nurse her through."

So out into December weather
They left Aunt Sue's house together
On a cold and rainy winter day
To nurse the former Widow Gray.

For days the woman lay in pain
Tortured by her fevered brain.
Aunt Sue sat by her; cooled her brow
Day and night; folks wondered how
She managed to endure so long
And help the one who did her wrong.

But finally there came a day
The woman's fever went away.
Aunt Sue came home; she'd done her part
Out of the goodness of her heart.

But she took to a fevered bed.
Three days later she was dead.
The doctor said she gave her life
To save her ex-husband's wife.

If you're in heaven and meet a saint
Ask her if she is my aunt.
For I'm sure she's somewhere there;
She'll have a gold star in her hair.

A Dubious Tale

It's so absurd it makes me feel
Quite like a nut just to reveal
The story I'm about to tell.
It's all about a guy in hell.

It seems he had a lot of strife
With one on earth he called his wife.
He got a gun and shot her dead.
The bullet ricocheted in his head.

He realized what he had done
As he fell on the smoking gun
But he knew it was too late:
He had stupidly sealed his fate.

And sure enough he went below
Where all wife-slayers go.
Someone down there let him in
To pay the price of his sin.

When he came to he figured out
Where he was, for all about
Were pitchforks. It was uncanny:
He knew no farmer had that many.

On top of this he smelled smoke.
He knew this couldn't be a joke:
Satan had pushed him o'er the brink
To get him in the Devil's clink.

And here he was with no escape!
Where was Superman with his cape?
How could he cope with brains satanic
When his own was gripped with panic?

Like a convict after sentence
He was stricken with repentance.
If he could live his life all over
He would stay completely sober.

Many things went through his mind
As he waited for the time
He would have to take his turn
To go into the fire and burn.

His agony was more than he
Ever imagined hell to be.
In a mood of deep despair
He offered up a sinner's prayer.

At that moment he heard screaming
It woke him up: he was just dreaming.
His wife was lying by his side!
Neither one of them had died.

But it taught him several lessons:
From now on he'll count his blessings
And he'll never contemplate
Killing folks, much less his mate.

The Family

Dear Lord, this house is home sweet home;
Each room is hallowed here.
The walls echo with reverence
The things we hold most dear.

The memories of togetherness
We've shared throughout the years
Are etched upon each heart in gold
Of laughter and of tears.

The years are passing swiftly . . .
The children almost grown;
Please, Lord, bless the harvest
Of seeds that we have sown.

In your eternal dwelling
No matter where we roam
May we assemble all as one . . .
A family coming home.

Love's Gift

Life was mundane — Incomplete.
God sent love, so dear, so sweet.
To bless that love — Oh, angels smile!
He sent the ultimate, a new-born child!

Aged Gardener

Each year I say, "This is my last;
The work's too hard; my youth has past."
But spring comes with its sun and rain;
Inspires me and I'm back again
Digging a hole; planting a row;
Tamping the seed down with my hoe;
Pulling a hose; bending my back;
Lifting a too-heavy fertilizer sack.

I groan and whimper like an injured pup
But feel ecstatic when the plants come up.

His Voice

Teach me to pray, Lord,
I asked of Him one day.
It seemed most important
The words that I say.

His response came softly,
"The answer that you seek
Is held within your heart . . .
I hear before you speak."

A Child's Anticipation Of Spring

I like to think of sunshine
When winter days are gray.
I often think of things I'll do
When winter goes away.

I'll run across the meadow;
Watch frisky lambs at play.
I'll watch a bluebird build a nest
When winter goes away.

I'll fly a kite up in the sky
In colors bright and gay.
I'll fish down in the pond again
When winter goes away.

If I didn't have the winter
To compare with days in May
I wouldn't appreciate spring
When winter goes away.

Condescension

When you're looking down your nose
At humble Tiny Tim
To others you appear to be
Somewhat less than him.

A Mother's Prayer

Bethlehem lay still and quiet
Beneath the winter's midnight skies
While a mother's tender touch
Soothed a new born baby's cries.

"Thank you, God," the mother said,
As she held her infant son.
"Make me worthy of Thy trust
In giving me Your Blessed One.

Give me wisdom to fullfill
The awesome role that You demand.
When at last the curtain falls
Give me faith to understand."

Ephemeral Delight

Tulips nodding in the wind
Beauty to my garden lend.
Colors moving to and fro —
Ballet dancers in the snow.

Petals float off in the air;
Soon my garden will be bare.
I stand and watch then while I can
As March winds I reprimand.

Life's Lesson

It seems like Fate just has a way
At times to crush us day by day.
But pain, I've learned, is part of life;
We have our joys, we have our strife.

The End Of The World once came to me
And sat on my doorstep. I could see
Nothing ahead but pain and dispair —
It was almost more than I could bear.

At first I thought I couldn't cope.
I cried a lot; had little hope
I'd ever feel like me again.
My whole world just turned to rain.

But finally as the time went by
I found that others, just like I,
Had sorrows, too; some far worse
Than those that seemed to me a curse.

T'was then I made a solemn vow
My attitude someway, somehow
I'd change. I'd feel less sorry for myself
And put my troubles on the shelf.

I'd smile more often; cry far less;
Extend a hand of friendliness
To those in need. And furthermore
I'd pray to God their faith restore.

At this time I became aware
I'd found the answer to my prayer.
By giving of myself I'd learned
That somehow this the tide had turned.

The world became a brighter place;
It all reflected in my face.
I had compassion for my friend
When his world came to an end.

No Christmas

Take the candles away, with their golden light,
Dispense with the holly and berries bright,
Silence the carols in the night,
    And there'd be
    No Christmas

Forget about friends and family dear,
Give no gifts to warm and cheer,
Send no cards far nor near,
    And there'd be
    No Christmas.

Lay no toys beneath a tree,
Disregard all charity,
Deny the Savior of you and me,
    And there'd be
    No Christmas

World Traveler

Wanderlust once touched my heart
And softly whispered,
"Come with me
There's a world to see!"
She took me by my naive hand
And over seas and over land
We traveled
To Singapore and old Bombay,
To Cairo, and Mandalay.

I followed ever where she led;
And sometimes when I'd gone to bed
She'd visit me;
Ever saying, "You are free,
Don't linger here,
Time is fleeting. Hurry on!"
I'd rise and dress;
The morning sun
Would find us gone.

Around the world, two times or more,
She led me;
Excited, breathlessly.
In every port I marveled at
Quaint customs, alien faiths,
Languages that obfuscate.

But through it all I came to see
People, universally,
Are the same. No matter where
Occurred their birth,
God put them there
To populate
Far corners of this planet earth.

A Lesson In Humility

Jim went to the nation's Capitol
A group to represent
While he was on the mission
He spoke with the president.

His family, left at home
Remembered him in prayer
Each day they knelt and asked
God keep him in His care.

Later, when Jim came home
His pride was evident
He asked, "Was it not great
I talked with the president?"

His four year old responded,
"Yes," he answered with a nod,
"But, Dad, while you were gone
We talked with GOD."

Second Thoughts

When I am chafed by petty things
And discontent with what life brings
Let me go then into the land
Where freedom is unknown to man.

Let me stand helpless in the shoes
Of a working man who cannot choose
His job, religion, or the way
In which he lives his life each day.

Let me wait hours in the line
For items that are hard to find
Then pay with sweat and blood the price
For things as commonplace as rice.

Let me work closely by the side
Of one who knows that he must hide
All literature or print
Not sanctioned by the government.

Let my sleep be tinged with fear
That government agents may come near
And knocking loudly they might say
That they are taking me away.

When I return to the USA
I'll think twice before I say
That I am bored or discontent.
I'll even praise our government.

For tyranny is a word
Others KNOW — we've only heard.

Simple Things

I like simple things
Like violets by an old rail fence,
The music of a babbling brook,
Forest trails, and woodland scents.

I'd forfeit wealth and luxury
For nature's sweet lifestyle.
I sometimes meditate
Life on a golden isle.

If heaven has streets of gold
And mansions fit for kings,
I hope God saves a corner
Filled with simple things.

What Might Have Been

The clock on the wall says midnight
And the embers cool and die
As I sit alone by the fireside
Dreaming of days gone by.

I guess it's only natural
For seventy year old men
To question the turn of Fate
And think of what might have been.

My thoughts go back to my childhood
When I was but nine years old
And I re-live the events
Of a story I've never told.

For I was a shy little lad
When Sue Smith moved next door
Our dads were business partners
In a small town grocery store.

Our homes were both two-story
On a quiet tree lined street
The distance between the windows
Was only sixty feet.

I saw her first one morning
In her window across the way
Trying to coax a bluebird
To eat from her hand and play.

"Don't be afraid," she said,
As she reached out a graceful arm
With a hand filled with sunflower seed
Hoping the bird to charm.

But the bird ignored her offer
As he basked in the sun's first ray
And I saw her disappointment
When the bluebird flew away.

But I was the one she charmed
As I watched from my bedroom blind
And secretly thought to myself
Someday I'd make her mine.

And as we played together
In the weeks and months ahead
I felt that God in heaven
Meant for us to wed.

One day on the backporch steps
I was whittling with my knife
When I looked up at her and said,
"Someday you'll be my wife."

"I know," she almost whispered
And turned away her head
In a wistful understanding
Of the words I had said.

Twelve sweet months went by
In innocent childhood play
Then summer came again . . .
I recall an August day.

Sue came down with fever
"Typhoid," said Old Doc Moore
I couldn't go in to see her
"Quarantined" was on the door.

I went to my upstairs window
Where I could view her room
I kept a daily vigil
But each day brought more gloom.

At three o'clock one morning
Having not slept through the night
I got up and went to the window
In her room was a pale lamplight.

There by her bed was her mother
Faithfully kneeling in prayer
I knew Sue must be failing
For Old Doc Moore was there.

He looked worn and haggard
As he sat by the side of her bed
When he covered Sue with a sheet
I knew my love was dead.

Sometime within the hour
Before the light of day
A hearse came to the sidewalk
And took my love away.

I watched with flowing tears
As the hearse drove out of sight
And I see it all again
As I sit alone tonight.

Now that I've reached the milestone
Of three score years and ten
I gaze into the ashes
And think of what might have been.

In Time Of Tears

Once when teardrops dimmed my eyes
God sent an angel in disguise
To comfort and hold my hand
'Til peace came to my heart again.

Today I said a reverent prayer
That God, through love, make me aware
Of one whose eyes with tears are dim
That I may go and comfort him.

The Valentine

The sad old man was seldom seen
Ten years he'd lived alone
His garden once was lush and green
His roses now were gone.

This day was passing slowly
The time just half past nine
Then the postman brought his mail . . .
A big red valentine.

He opened it with trembling hands
His vision was not good
But the message that it brought
Was clearly understood.

His face lit up like sunshine
His eyes like stars in heaven
For Jane, the sender, lived next door . . .
Jane was only seven.

Reflection

Heartache is not easy to forget,
It follows us persistantly . . . and yet,
Had I not known bleak moments of dispair
How could I know the pain a heart can bear?

No Time To Write

"I'll get a letter in the mail,"
You tell yourself, "without fail.
But, oh, I hear the telephone;
Right now the letter I'll postpone."

A neighbor says, "Let's go to town
Just for fun; we'll shop around."
You answer her, "That's fine with me."
And rush to get your purse and key.

The day gets by; it's suppertime.
The letter somehow slips your mind.
Day by day things go the same;
Procrastination is the game.

At a distance there is one
Waiting for a note to come.
When the postman passes by
She wipes a teardrop from her eye.

Reader, pause and close your eyes
For a moment realize
The situation could be worse . . .
IT COULD BE IN DIRECT REVERSE.

The Relic

Pages yellowed, long forgotten,
Printed many years before,
She, perchance, may come upon it
Browsing through a used book store.

Tenderly she'll turn the pages
Reading silently each line.
She may smile with gentle reverence
At the simple words of mine.

She will muse upon the title,
Briefly written, "To You From Me."
It is not improbable
The words speak to her personally.

Prompted by her human instinct
To share joy with another,
To the clerk she'll smile and say,
"This author is my great-grandmother."

She will wipe the dusty cover
Faded by the years of time
And she'll buy her priceless treasure . . .
Worldly value — one thin dime.

NOTE:
Kerri Darlene Hughes, the Author's only great-granddaughter, is Age 3.

Biographical Sketch

MELBA HUGHES

Born the third child in a family of seven children, raised in sawmill camps and small rural communities, finished highschool at Cottonton, AL 1932.

I've lived in eight states and Europe.

I'm a great grandmother.

My hobbies are in the creative arts.

I like Emerson's essays, Tennyson's poetry, and Dickens' stories.

My favorite past-time — working cryptograms.

I take people into my home and into my heart.

For additional copies of TO YOU FROM
ME by Melba Hughes, send $8.45 (postpaid)
to Rainbow Books, Order Department,
Moore Haven, FL 33471-1069